simply pink

# PAULA PRYKE
# *simply pink*

photography by Polly Wreford

**RIZZOLI**
NEW YORK

For Elizabeth and Anne
and all those who believe in the magic of pink!

First published in the United States of
America in 2009 by
Rizzoli International Publications, Inc.
300 Park Avenue South
New York, NY 10010
www.rizzoliusa.com

Originally published in the United Kingdom
in 2009 by
Jacqui Small LLP,
7 Greenland Street
London NW1 0ND

Publisher  Jacqui Small
Editorial Manager  Lesley Felce
Designer  Maggie Town
Editor  Sian Parkhouse
Production  Peter Colley

2009 2010 2011 2012 / 10 9 8 7 6 5 4 3 2 1

ISBN: 978-0-8478-3178-4

Library of Congress Control Number:
2008934689

Printed in China

# contents

# my passion for pink

MY LOVE AFFAIR with the color pink started in childhood but has endured and intensified as I have matured. I still prefer pink to any other color. There is something about the color that intrigues me. It has such a wide color spectrum and I find I have a very emotional reaction to it. At one level it soothes and beguiles me and makes me feel just a little more rosy inside. It is a happy color, a fun color and above all a slightly magical color. It can be calming, soothing, and gentle or it can be outrageous, loud, and arresting. Pink can suggest many things: femininity, youthfulness, innocence, delicacy, romance and yet it can also be very dominant, bold and sexy!

I feel extremely privileged to be able to work professionally with flowers and one of the most motivating forces for me is working with the colors of nature. In our everyday life we are now very influenced by the color trends of the season. Color predictors may suggest seasonal colors that reflect world events and the mood of the times and marketing gurus may more cynically present others to us.

Whatever the trends for the last few years, working so closely with clients' color choices I can confirm that for the last five years we have been going through a very pink phase, with it being by far the most requested color and the preferred wedding choice. As a result of its popularity, there has been an enormous influx of new varieties of flowers produced for the cut-flower trade in the pink color spectrum. We are definitely currently in the pink, and long may it continue!

ABOVE  Pink ranunculus—my favorite flower.

pink inspirations

THIS PAGE My pink cottage garden favorites include *Clematis* 'Anna,' *Cirsium rivulare* 'Atropurpureum,' valerian, foxgloves, lupins, 'Handel' and 'Gertrude Jekyll' roses and candy pink *Campanula medium* 'Champion Pink,' with flowering stems of honeysuckle.

# garden bounty

**FOR THE LAST FOUR YEARS** I have been living outside London and reconnecting with gardening. I am not a good garden designer because I want to have one of everything and I like my garden to be so packed with flowers that it is like walking through one of my arrangements. I also prefer it to be slightly wild and natural, too, and I tend to let the dominant plants have their way with the weaker ones rather than imposing my own will. These collections of pink flowers were harvested from my own patch in the early morning before the commute to London. Valerian is a self-sown flower in my garden, but I have come to love it since I have found it to be such a useful filler for my flower arrangements, and it has a good vase life. Honeysuckle is a passion, and I have at least five different varieties in my garden, but it does not last well as a cut flower.

TOP RIGHT I think clematis is very underrated as a cut flower—here the pale pink variety 'Anna' is arranged with lupins and valerian.

MAIN PICTURE I am a huge admirer of foxgloves, particularly when they grow wild and are not under the watchful eye of a gardener. These tall spires of quite exotic looking, delicate bell-shaped flowers with spotted throats make good seasonal cut flowers in late spring and early summer.

LEFT A selection of old fashioned "pinks," known in Tudor times as gillyflowers. In Shakespeare's *The Winter's Tale*, Polixenes urges Perdita 'Then make your garden rich in gillyvors.'

RIGHT The quintessential rose, 'Gertrude Jekyll' is simply the best. I love the color and the shape.

*"Roses are incredibly sensual and I would not be without them in my garden."*

# my favorite rose

IT IS VERY HARD FOR ME to offer up just one favorite pink rose when there are so many I adore and order from my suppliers each week, but one that has endured and been constant for the last 15 years or so is the South American rose 'Anna.' It has a very lovely shape and color and the inside of the rose is just slightly paler than the outside. It reminds me of the highest quality ice cream—the color is so attractive it looks creamy and almost good enough to eat! South American roses are packed in 25s rather than the usual 20s and they are usually rather less uniform in length. Their heads are packed at different heights to make maximum room for the air freight and when they are unpacked they need reviving by re-cutting about 2 inches off the bottom of the stem with a diagonal cut, and letting them regain their strength in water mixed with flower food with their packaging still on. After 24 hours we remove the packaging and any outer petals of the rose head that have been damaged by the wrapping. They look just perfect massed together on their own.

OPPOSITE  A large hand-tied posy of 'Anna' roses—the perfect bouquet to celebrate the arrival of a baby girl.

THIS PAGE  The  color variation is what makes 'Anna' so perfect to me, with its gradations from the creamy bud opening into pink outer petals.

THIS PAGE Everlasting pea, feverfew, blackberry, valerian, wild teasels, Queen Anne's lace, sweet cicely, veronica and musk mallow are each given their own milk bottle vase, and the collection is bound together with gardener's twine.

# wildflower hunt

**IN RETROSPECT** I think my obsession with flowers started when I was about five or six when I picked wildflowers in the water meadows around my parents' home in Suffolk, England. Observing flowers in the wild is a huge inspiration for me and it leads to a more holistic approach to flower arranging. The shape of the flower, its habitat, and the way that it is mixed with other colors have all informed my work. While out walking, if you come across a carpet of bluebells or a scattering of foxgloves in a leafy glade you are struck by the power of massing one type of flower together. The simplicity of flowers in nature is also arresting and always central to my work. For me the simpler the design the better it is, as you are drawn more to the stars of the arrangement, the flowers themselves. The natural curiosity of a child to collect a group of random flowers and place them together in an old jelly jar is simplicity at its best.

THIS PAGE It is amazing what treasures a country walk can yield. This collection of self-sown garden and wildflowers demonstrates that Mother Nature is as big a fan of the color pink as I am!

INSET BELOW One of the joys of working with flowers is that there are always new varieties appearing, and with the change of the seasons there is a constant roving menu of plant material. This helps to keep my work fresh and evolving. Every now and then a new rose comes along and leads you to new combinations. This dusky pink 'Two Faces+' rose has been a recent muse.

# paisley pinks

**THE SETTING AND INTERIOR** of a room is central to the selection of plant material and containers. Table linen in particular is often chosen in collaboration with the flowers' decorations, sometimes to match or tone, and always to make the most of the central arrangement. On some occasions I may be sent a swatch of fabric for a bridesmaid's dress or for a tablecloth from an event planner, and I will take it along to the wholesale flower market early in the morning and begin to collect flowers and foliages which complement the swatch. When the event is in a marquee or a simple room like a modern museum you can often use patterned cloths to great effect because the interior is essentially blank and does not fight with the table linen. Sometimes the colors and the style of the fabric will more directly affect my choice of design. Here the swirl pattern of the paisley invited me to use a curly sage green boat container and then use a collection of very textural and blowsy shapes to fill it.

THIS PAGE Blowsy 'Shirley Temple' peonies have been mixed with silver eryngium, *Rosa* 'Two Faces+,' dark burgundy *Cotinus coggygria* 'Royal Purple,' silver *Brachyglottis*, 'Sunshine,' 'Phillipa' garden roses, and sweet peas. The swirling shapes of the petals reflect the movement in the fabric design.

# rustic pitchers and cans

I HAVE OFTEN BEEN ASKED which comes first in the design process, the container or the flowers. In my own home I nearly always choose the flowers and then select the vase from my vast collection. However, often a selection of flowers will suggest a particular type of vase or the container itself will inspire me to put together a design. Rustic pitchers and watering cans are great inspirational forces and invite me to spiral cottage favorites into country bunches. I also love old cooking pots and jars, particularly in earthy tones, such as antique oil pots from the Provence region of France or earthenware kitchen bowls. Antique carafes and jars can also make great vases. Many of these containers have wide bases and narrower tops, which are the best shape for hand-tied bouquets and display the flower heads well.

OPPOSITE I filled this pink enameled watering can with blue and pink love-in-a-mist (the pink variety *Nigella* 'Pink Power' is new as a cut flower), *Astilbe* 'Erica,' pale pink stocks, a new variety of pale lilac scabious, and a new double daisy *Aster* 'Pink Pearl.'

THIS PAGE I love the shape of this enamel pitcher which, when filled, has a wide enough mouth to create a good spread of flowers. Here it is filled with *Alchemilla mollis*, *Consolida ajacis*, rose-colored eustoma, two-tone antirrhinum, and the wonderful scented garden rose 'Evelyn.'

rustic pitchers and cans    **21**

THIS PAGE A hand-tied posy of 'Barcelona' tulips, aqua-packed in cellophane, sits in a sequinned bag. We make lots of this type of arrangement for bridesmaids' posies, as they are easy to carry. Pink roses would work equally well in this bag.

# bags and baskets

**FLOWERS HAVE BEEN ARRANGED** in baskets since the beginning of modern floristry, which has its origins in the early 20th century. Baskets were originally an inexpensive natural container made from bamboo or willow, which complemented the flowers. Arranging flowers in bags became fashionable about ten years ago when it became a new way to market "to-go" flowers. At about the same time, bags filled with flowers for special events and weddings became a new take on an old theme and one that has become very central to my trademark look. Taking new accessories and using them to originate new flower arrangements has added a very feminine look to my work, and these accessories have contributed greatly to the inspiration of new designs.

THIS PAGE The brightly toned woven basket was filled with the guelder rose *Viburnum opulus* 'Roseum,' asters, and 'Cristian' spray roses. This is an ideal gift to take with you if you are arriving at an event, as the hostess needs to do nothing with it other than display it!

LEFT  This sequined flower handbag captivated me, as flower shapes are a very important inspiration in my designs. Here the round shape of a daisy whose petals radiate from one central point had inspired a handbag designer.

OPPOSITE  This was my interpretation of the daisy bag in flowers. A posy of pink carnations *Dianthus* 'Farida' encircles an echinops head studded with pink pearl-headed pins. A design in which nature imitates fashion imitating nature!

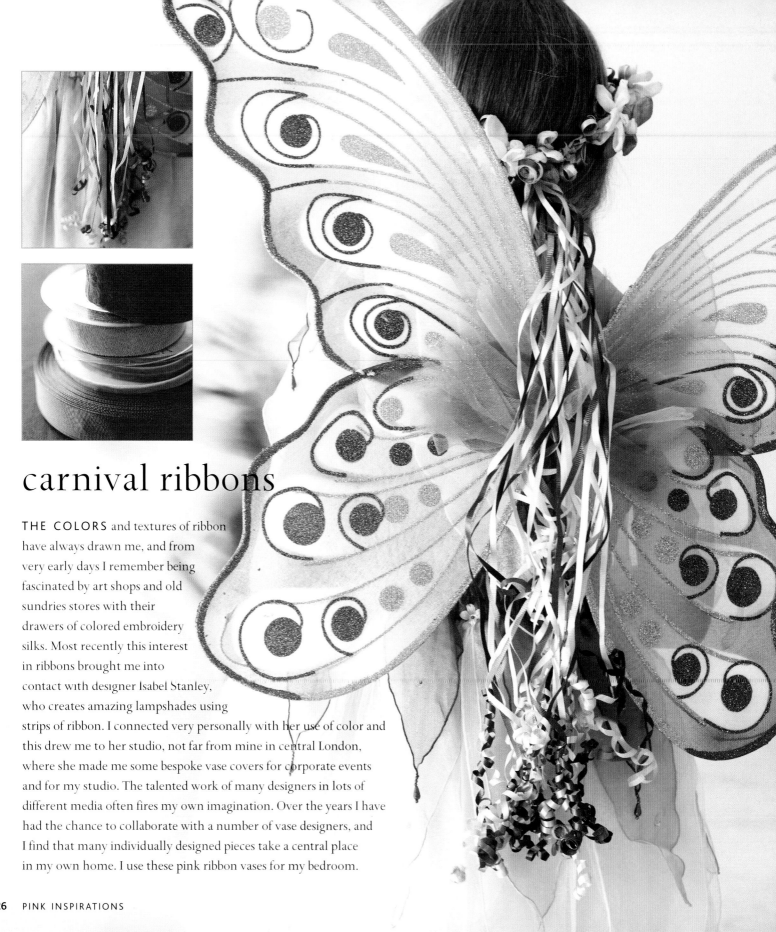

# carnival ribbons

**THE COLORS** and textures of ribbon have always drawn me, and from very early days I remember being fascinated by art shops and old sundries stores with their drawers of colored embroidery silks. Most recently this interest in ribbons brought me into contact with designer Isabel Stanley, who creates amazing lampshades using strips of ribbon. I connected very personally with her use of color and this drew me to her studio, not far from mine in central London, where she made me some bespoke vase covers for corporate events and for my studio. The talented work of many designers in lots of different media often fires my own imagination. Over the years I have had the chance to collaborate with a number of vase designers, and I find that many individually designed pieces take a central place in my own home. I use these pink ribbon vases for my bedroom.

OPPOSITE, MAIN PICTURE AND INSET ABOVE  I was given these carnival headdresses at the San Antonio Children's Fiesta in Texas, and they have often inspired me to use long ribbons in my fresh headdress designs.

OPPOSITE, INSET BELOW  I love the textures and finishes of these ribbons, and I have spools of them in my studio. THIS PAGE  This tall ribbon vase is filled with *Stephanandra, Cotinus coggygria* 'Royal Purple,' *Lilium* 'Medusa,' *Paeonia lactiflora* 'Karl Rosenfield,' amaranthus, *Dahlia* 'Karma Choc,' and the small *Allium sphaerocephalon*.

THIS PAGE Pink aquatic aggregates have been swirled into this glass fishbowl and then topped with a spiraled hand-tied posy of green amaranthus, blue 'Whisper' eryngiums, Germini gerberas, *Alchemilla mollis*, garden roses, and a collar of the coral fern *Gleichenia polypodioides*. Wired seashells have been placed through the design with pink reel wire.

OPPOSITE Nature is a great teacher and inspiration about color, texture, and good design, no more so than in a collection of perfectly formed seashells.

# seashells and sand

**PICKING UP SEASHELLS** on the beach is as natural to me as picking wildflowers while on a walk. Their textures, colors, and shapes are fascinating and their natural tones work well with plant material. I often like to work with them on their own and, using a glue gun, will make them into wreaths. At Christmastime we often gild them and add shells to trees, garlands, and seasonal wreaths. Using sand, stones, and other aggregates is an inexpensive way of customizing a container in a color or a pattern, as shown here. A cylinder-shaped glass vase was placed into a fishbowl. The gap was filled with swirls of colored aggregates and sand, and then a few special shells were wired into a hand-tied design.

THIS PAGE A selection of candies
that make perfect partners for pink
flowers: bon-bons, alphabet candies,
sherbert disks, and jellybeans.

OPPOSITE A straight-sided glass dish
was filled with an inner liner containing
floral foam and filled with colored mints.
The flowers include 'Revival,' 'Prima
Donna,' and 'Ilios!' roses, pink veronica,
pink and peach ranunculus, 'Gipsy
Queen' hyacinths, and green
amaranthus. The little green balls are the
flax *Linum usitatissimum*—this is grown
mostly for dried flower supply.

# candies

I HAVE BEEN USING CANDIES as accessories to my designs for well over 15 years. I think I am drawn to the colors and the combination they offer, which is either very pastel or can be very artificial if a lot of food dye has been used. Mostly we use the pastel colors for weddings and christenings and the more brightly colored sweets for bar mitzvahs. Sometimes we use the sweets on their own. I once decorated a family and friends' Christmas party for a major banking group at the Royal Opera House in Covent Garden, London, just using a truckload of multicolored liqorice candies and lots of hot glue. I recently made cones of brightly colored hard-boiled candies for the children's tables of a bar mitzvah, while the highly dyed harlequin-colored Happy roses were used en masse on all the adult tables.

pink
by design

LEFT Single heads of bright pink ranunculus are arranged in small water-holding phials in delicate banana skin bags, allowing the innate beauty of the flower form to be highlighted.

RIGHT Posies of ranunculus edged with galax leaves are ready for two lucky bridesmaids to carry. Ranunculus can make a great alternative to roses for wedding flowers, as they have greater longevity and hold their shape well.

# favorite flowers

What first attracted me to change my career to one in floristry was the love of flowers, pure and simple, both in my garden, in the countryside, and more exotic cut flowers, and, not surprisingly, many of my favorites are available in many shades of pink.

**RANUNCULUS** These pretty blooms have remained in the top position as my favorite flower since I started to work professionally with flowers over 20 years go. Initially I was attracted to the multicolored mix of brightly colored ranunculus grown in Cornwall that arrive in Covent Garden market around the time of my birthday in late April. Over the years these flowers have been improved enormously by hybridization and I adore the large-headed pink Clooney and the spotted Cappuccino varieties.

The main reason for my obsession with these blooms is that they are at their most graceful and gorgeous the day before they expire. When you first place ranunculus in water they are simply a bunch of wild-looking stems with good-looking tight, round blooms. After 24 hours in water they will start to rearrange themselves, drawn by the sunlight, into a more gorgeous design and their heads start to swell a little. By the end of the week they will have opened fully, then the petals unfold and take on a translucency as if they are about to take off from the stem. I think they look better and better each day and then, just when they reach their most beautiful, they are gone, reminding me always of the transient beauty of the natural world.

*"The scent of sweet peas is the quintessential fragrance of the summer months."*

**SWEET PEA** The English Romantic poet John Keats described these beautiful flowers: "*Here are sweet peas, on tip-toe for a flight: | With wings of gentle flush o'er delicate white, | And taper fingers catching at all things, | To bind them all about with tiny rings.*" Growing sweet peas is a perennial pleasure because they have such an interesting habit and they produce handfuls of beautiful fragrant flowers for several months.

As a cut flower they have been enormously improved and the single-colored bunches that are sold commercially are treated post-harvest to give them greater longevity in the vase and engender them less susceptible to petal loss. For the florist, sweet peas start around Valentine's Day, with a peak in the middle of the year before they start to disappear in September.

ABOVE Sweet peas can get a little lost when mixed with other flowers so I prefer to use them on their own, massed together for their scent; on this occasion the whole arrangement was repeated for maximum impact.

**ROSE** There are so many varieties of roses available commercially each week, and in the last three years there has been a huge development in the range of pink roses on sale. At the cerise end of the scale I love 'Milano,' a long-lasting and tall pink rose which perfectly suits gloriosa lilies. 'Aqua!' is a mid-pink rose, which has been developed especially for the trade and does not have any thorns, which is a huge time-saver for busy florists. Large-headed 'Sweet Avalanche+' is a favorite pale rose and perfect for weddings. The aptly named 'Barbie' is the perfect color for little girls, as is 'Ballet,' being stronger and more the color of bubble gum than a tutu. New mid-pink large-headed roses which are among my favorites are 'Revival,' 'Luxuria!,' 'Keano,' and 'Lyvera!' 'Belle Rose' is a subtle honey pink rose with a darker pink center and 'Two Faces+' is a dusty brown rose that is hugely popular. There are also some fabulous spray roses in the pink range. 'Pepita' is pale pink, with 'Magic Pepita' and 'Romantic Pepita' being stronger colors. 'Lovely Lydia' is a peach-pink spray rose and 'Mimi Eden' is cream on the outside and pink inside, and most resembles a garden rose.

LEFT  A selection of pink and red roses demonstrates the beauty of the flower: a neat domed hand-tied bouquet of 'Grand Prix,' 'Milano,'and 'Cool Water!' roses is edged with curled aspidistra leaves.

RIGHT  'Blue Pacific,' 'Amalia,' 'Grand Prix,' and 'Titanic' roses are edged with camellia leaves and a woven collar of intertwined red Iranian dogwood and green broom. Swirls of green wire orbit the bunch to give it a wilder look.

ABOVE Pliable stems of birch and pussy willow, with their soft buds and catkins just emerging, have been twisted and woven into a basket encircling a posy of 'Blue Diamond' tulips, for a striking spring arrangement.

**TULIP** I am passionate about tulips both in my garden and in my floral designs. They are one of the most versatile of all the spring bulbs. The range is quite enormous and the supply to the cut flower trade almost continuous, but the best months are between November and May. 'Angélique' is a double-flowering bluish pink tulip that grows paler as it opens to reveal a soft inner lining. 'Foxtrot' and 'Peach Blossom' are similar in shape to 'Angélique' and are in fact pink beauties. 'Barcelona' is a fuchsia pink mid-season tulip and 'Lilynita' is a stunning rose pink with a purple flush on the long pointed petals. It is reminiscent of the lily-flowered tulips, of which 'China Pink' and 'Mariette' are my favorites.

However my current favorites of the moment are the lovely fringed tulips, with their clearly defined crystalline petal edges. They are a joy to behold. 'Huis ten Bosch' is the most beautiful fringed variety, but I also love the two-toned 'Sweet Love', which is a soft lilac rose pink. Great parrot pinks include 'Groenland,' 'China Town,' and 'Weber's Parrot.' For a more raspberry pink color plump for 'Estella Rÿnveld' or 'Fantasy.' 'Picture' is a lovely lilac rose tulip with pointed petals that turn outwards, making it very distinctive. Finally, one of the finest pink tulips is undoubtedly 'Pink Diamond' which is a beautiful shade of pink—the color of phlox—and is both a great garden tulip and a superb cut flower.

**GERBERA** Although gerberas are not such personal favorites as the other flowers in this section I have included them because they come up time and time again in my work. They are available in so many wonderful colors, of which pink is one amazing example. You can buy a gerbera in just about any shade of pink any week of the year. It can be used in all types of floristry and, with the smaller germini varieties as well, there are over 150 colors to select from.

MAIN PICTURE Individual Germini gerberas repeated in small tank vases make an inexpensive floral statement. These colorful daisies, which originated in Africa, are now grown in all the major flower producing regions of the world all year round.

INSET This massed topiary of pink gerberas is a less expensive way of achieving a lot of impact at an event. Here a base of eucalyptus and skimmia are the background for these showy pink flowers. They have been raised off the table using a spray painted birch pole.

LEFT The muted tones of pale pink with dusty pinks and browns is one one of my favorite combinations in mid-summer. Here 'Sarah Bernhardt' peonies are hand tied with brown 'Amnésia,' pale pink 'Sweet Avalanche+,' and dusty pink 'Two Faces+' roses, a mixture of poppy seed heads, photinia, *Alchemilla mollis* and green dill *Anethum graveleons*. A little pink water dye has been added to the fishbowl to give a rosy glow.

# shades of pink

It is the versatility in the shades of pink that make it the most important color for me in my floral designing. Mixing the right colors is like carefully choreographing a group of dancers to create someting that is both graceful and entertaining. It's relatively easy to do the first, but making a combination achieve the second is either an innate skill or gift, or it can be the process of long endeavor, and trial and error.

**SOFTLY SOFTLY** We can all follow the recipe for cupcakes but some people's just taste so much better than others'. With experience you get to learn good combinations, but for me all the fun is in creating new ones and not always using the same safe selections. When arranging soft tones you have to be very careful to balance the intensity of each color or be clever with your use of foliage to accentuate each color value. Once you mix white into a combination it becomes very diluted, so I either like to use it quite strongly, as in the striped design, or to use it with just one color. In a pink and white arrangement be careful to make sure the pink is less dominant so that it does not distract the eye too much.

RIGHT I always feel slightly wary of specifying Japanese knotweed from the Dutch auction after reading how invasive it has been as an imported plant—however it does have a great texture when the stems are cut open. Here small lengths edge a Perspex tray of 'Avalanche+,' pink 'Sweet Avalanche+,' and 'Peach Avalanche+' roses.

LEFT 'Pink Cappuccino' ranunculus, 'Marshmallow' and 'Barbie' roses, and 'First Class' tulips have been mixed with the white spring blossom of *Viburnum tinus*. The vase is lined with the cushiony shapes of marshmallows.

**SUGAR CANDY PINKS** Working with a candy pink color palette is a more delicate art than with pastel shades or pinks from the loud range of color. Pink is at its prettiest and most feminine when it is in mid palette and I am particularly inspired by this in early spring, when the blossom is out and there are lots of great tulips and ranunculus to use, and also again in mid summer when the peonies, sweet peas, campanula, and stocks all start to beguile me. The soft tones work well on their own or when lifted and accentuated by the use of dark foliages or lighter and brighter hues. They love gray foliage and they also adore lime green. You have to be very careful not to use too much white, as that saps the subtleties, and you also have to be very wary of yellow and any variegated foliages. In a mixed palette, using more than two colors, I would leave out the white, preferring cream or vanilla as they are more subtle and complementary.

THIS PAGE I adore these 'Gertrude Jekyll' roses mixed with 'Prima Donna' and 'Super Green' roses, sprigs of lime green *Alchemilla mollis*, pale blue nigella, candy pink nerines, campanula, and 'Sarah Bernhardt' peonies. Here the palette of the round sherbet candies has inspired the color of these summer flowers.

**HOT PINKS** The brightest and most garish pink is always the most fun! It's the slightly outrageous relative, the one that pushes the boundaries too far. The one that most people love or hate. It knows no mediocrity, it's in your face. It is the adolescent of the pink family. It demands attention and takes no hostages, only prisoners. I adore this pink and I find this color invaluable as an accent color. I don't want to surround myself with it, but I do need a little burst of it every now and then. I love hot pink roses, peonies, celosia, gerberas, dahlias, and, most of all, exotic tendrils of climbing gloriosa heads.

LEFT Bright pink 'Serena' gerberas, gloriosa, 'Milano' roses, and sprigs of fuchsia pink sisal have been added in heavy groups to a ring around a glass bowl. The pink is contrasted against orange roses and leucospermums, purple eustoma, and silver brunia and coral fern foliages. Birds of paradise flowers and twisted willow stems add height.

RIGHT Grouping flowers together is one way to make more dramatic color combinations. Here pink 'Barbie' and peach 'Prima Donna' roses have been mixed with photinia foliage, *Viburnum opulus* 'Roseum,' blue hyacinths, and bright pink celosia.

**BRIGHT PINK MIXES EASILY WITH ANY COLOR** My favorite combinations tend to change with the season. In spring I major on bright pink with lilacs, pale blue, and acid greens. As the summer unfolds I use a lot more pink with purple and deep blue. By the time we get to mid summer I tend to go for even brighter combinations, mixing sunflowers with bright pink roses, celosia, and gloriosa, adding green dill and yellow achillea into the mix. In the fall I will be drawn to using pink with orange and purples, and at Christmastime I use bright pink with red and orange. If you add gold to this combination you get a rich but modern look for your festive arrangements.

OPPOSITE PAGE: ABOVE LEFT Pink bouvardia, cymbidium orchids, calla lilies, and mid-pink 'Beauty by Oger' roses have been added to viburnum blossom and ivy berries in a glass vase lined with slices of cut lime. ABOVE RIGHT Dried lavender has been tied around a basket and then topped with a creamy mixture of garden roses in pinks and creams. BELOW LEFT Bright pink 'Milano' roses, *Celosia argentea* var. *cristata* 'Bombay Pink,' and 'Aisha' gerberas are contrasted with orange flower heads and arranged in a bowl of sliced oranges. BELOW RIGHT A perennially favorite color combination of pink, lilac, and green. Pink dahlias, roses, eustoma, hydrangea, and astilbe are spiraled with green *Viburnum opulus* 'Roseum,' fountain grasses, and *Alchemilla mollis*.

THIS PAGE Big blowsy 'Kansas' peonies have been mixed with celosia and 'Serena' gerberas, with cream peonies and lime green viburnum and *Alchemilla mollis* to give this a fresh and vibrant summer feel.

# floral drama

Massing flowers together or heavily grouping them creates great visual impact and is a key way to create contemporary-feeling arrangements.

**CREATING HEIGHT** A tall vase is essential for making a dramatic display. These can either be used on a pedestal to give further height, or they can be placed on the center of a table to create a grand impression at a party or special venue. Ideally for tables I tend to use clear glass vases with thin stems, so a fluted glass shape is my preferred vase. I often decorate it with fruit, candies, or petals and use layers of cellophane in between which, when filled with water, gives the effect of ice.

LEFT Groups of elegantly curving *Nectaroscordum siculum, Anthurium* 'Nexia' tucked into the top of the vase, and *Zantedeschia* 'Aurora' tied with bright pink banana rope create an arrestingly sculptural display.

RIGHT 'Pink Panther' and 'Karl Rosenfield' peonies are interspersed with *Alchemilla mollis* and trails of asparagus fern. To add further texture and color, the clear glass vase has been layered with cherries and faux summer berries, alternated with cut clear cellophane.

floral drama  **53**

LEFT  Scented stocks, massed together with a collar of twisted allium stems, demonstrate their full palette of pinks through to purple. Although you can buy stocks all the year round they are less expensive in their natural season.

OPPOSITE, LEFT  Phalaenopsis orchids hand-tied with monstera leaves are balanced on the top of a vase filled with cut phalaenopsis heads and coiled decorative pink aluminum wire.

OPPOSITE, RIGHT  One of my favorite vases is this slightly flared cylinder vase, as it is a very elegant shape. I have collected them over the years in many colors and we have them in clear glass, white, black, and pale pink. Here a big "football" sphere of green floral foam has been placed onto the top of the vase and then filled with pale pink to mid-pink 'Heaven,' 'Barbie,' 'Blushing Akito,' 'Video,' and cream 'Talea+' roses.

**MASSED IMPACT** In the wild if you see a mass of one type of wildflower it is very arresting. The site of a carpet of buttercups in a meadow, a field of bright red poppies, a swirl of ox-eye daisies on the side of a freeway, all make very dramatic eye-catching displays. In the same way the use of one type of flower en masse for an event is very impressive. Two flowers that we use very often in this way are roses and phalaenopsis orchids. Roses work well because they can create quite sculptural effects and with the range of colors available you can always find one to match your event. Phalaenopsis orchids do not combine visually with other flowers, but look stunning and simply opulent when hand-tied together and used in tall glass vases. When flowers are in their natural season you can often buy them much more cheaply, and so this is a good time to try out the massed look without breaking the bank.

LEFT This large glossy pink urn is filled with flowering pink rhododendron, hydrangea, white lilac, spiraea, gladioli, larkspur, hanging amaranthus, dicentra, peonies, and the guelder rose *Viburnum opulus* 'Roseum.'

RIGHT Tall spires of pale pink eremurus rise from a dome of pink 'Amalia,' 'Two Faces+,' and 'Blushing Akito' roses.

**GRAND DESIGNS** For large arrangements you generally need to order longer length flowers, or create some structure to secure flower heads onto. For huge installations this may be a purpose-made structure such as an arch or a topiary shape. But if you wish to create a large arrangement using natural flowers for an urn on a pedestal or vase you will need to specify tall flowers. At most times of the year there are lots of flowers 30–40 inches tall, and on a trip to the huge flower auctions in the Netherlands at any time of the year visitors will be amazed by the sheer range in sizes on offer in many varieties. Usually for a more traditional design one would start to get height and volume by using some very tall foliages, establishing an outline with the greenery first, and then adding the flowers. I often begin with tall spires of flowers such as pink gladioli, maybe delphinium or larkspur, and then working in the larger-headed focal flowers, such as peonies and hydrangea, and finally the fillers to lighten dark spaces in the arrangement.

# decorative containers

One of my trademarks has been to use containers that were not originally intended for flowers. Platters, fruit bowls, handbags, and even lampshades are all everyday objects that I have used in my floral designs, most frequently in pink!

**CROCKERY** Twenty years ago the containers for flower arranging were very defined. They were site specific or range specific, and were usually more decorative than practical. The necks were too thin for great flower arrangements and in the main the proportions were too mean for a decent bunch of flowers. Many were actually not conducive to good flower arranging because they were too fussy or decorative. Vases were designed by potteries without much thought of how the flower arranger was going to create a good design. Some ceramic vases were designed by great floral designers, such as Constance Spry in the mid-20th century, but as this was before floral foam had been invented most relied on the use of chicken wire or had a flower rose inside to help position the flowers. The use of foam and hand-tying of flowers has opened up the possibilities for arrangements, and any shape can now be filled with the use of contemporary techniques and floral sundries.

RIGHT  A simple flower bottle from British ceramics designer Emma Bridgewater, appropriately decorated with the words "pink flowers," makes the perfect partner for a natural arrangement of 'Kansas' peonies.

FAR RIGHT  A group of plain white mugs—the type that most of us have in our kitchen closet—looks stunning when filled with domed hand-tied posies of multi-hued sweet William.

*"The perfect container is like the perfect outfit—you find it when you are not actually looking for it."*

LEFT The soft tones of this pale pink Provençal cooking bowl inspired this arrangement of *Cosmos atrosanguineus* 'Black Beauty,' standard carnations, ligularia leaves, blackberries, and 'Sweet Avalanche' roses.

BELOW The perfect desk accessory— *Dianthus* 'Farida' with *Alchemilla mollis*, 'Leila' Germini gerberas, and *Origanum* 'Gijsie' in an iconic Pantone pink mug.

**BASKETS** It is quite amazing to think that only about 20 years ago the main containers for flower arrangements for special occasions were baskets. These were mostly inexpensive blond bamboo baskets made in China and people who received a lot of flowers always had a massive collection of flower baskets that had been used only once. In the main at that time they had long handles for carrying and were a feature of home, wedding, and even funeral flowers. I am always on the look out for quirky equivalents to give an old theme a new look, and improvements in dying techniques have led to a huge variety of color in baskets. The expansion of plastic manufacturing has also given birth to lots of other highly colored products that hold water and make great containers for flower designs.

RIGHT  A deep pink woven bamboo basket is filled with *Chenopodium quinoa* 'Carina,' *Nigella* 'Pink Power,' *Alchemilla mollis*, cotinus foliage, and *Asclepias* 'Amalia.'

LEFT Red dogwood has been arranged round a central block of floral foam standing in the center of a straight-sided glass dish. A tight dome of 'Cool Water!,' 'Black Baccara,' and 'Amalia' roses has been placed into the center and then a collar of *Muehlenbeckia* vine arranged around the edge.

**NATURAL DECORATION** I love to make my own containers or to adapt simple containers so that you can create a more sculptural look. When I started my career in floristry this was often about adapting plastic containers and baskets, either by using double-sided tape around plastic bowls, or wire or glue around baskets. The basket on the right has been adapted with some glycerine leaves, some brown flocked Sumatra twigs, and the use of some wire and a hot glue gun. The left-hand arrangement could be created using a container within a container or by placing twigs around a large round of floral foam. These two designs are essentially rustic, but the massed rose heads make the one on the left look slightly more contemporary than the one on the right.

RIGHT This basket has been covered with brown glycerined leaves and flocked Sumatra twigs, and then filled with a hand-tied bouquet of rudbeckia, red skimmia, oak and galax leaves, with 'Beauty by Oger,' 'Halloween' and 'Aroma' roses, and miniature pink anthuriums.

LEFT This summer urn is filled with huge 'Coral Charm' peonies, grouped 'Amalia,' 'Marrakech,' and 'Peppermint' roses, with *Viburnum opulus* berries, *Photina* x *fraseri* 'Red Robin,' and *Astrantia major* 'Claret' as the filler material.

**URNS** Urns and flower arrangements go together rather like the egg and spoon. You can see in museums all over the world how urns and vases have evolved and there is lots to inspire the flower arranger. Most urns have a rustic feel, being made from stone, iron, or terracotta, and this is very sympathetic to plant material. Many of the ones we use for weddings are now made from fiberglass so they are lighter to move about than traditional urns, and there are also lots of new plastic versions on the market. Heavy metal urns are suitable to anchor heavy constructions such as the topiaries shown on these pages. I also find that heavy table urns are useful because they raise the flowers up in the center of the table so they are not obscured by the wine and water glasses. Also their weight makes them less attractive to take home at the end of the event when we are trying to recover all our props! The classic urn shape is also now made in glass and recently there have been lots of colored versions, including the bright pink one seen on page 56.

RIGHT Pink can give a traditional Christmas spruce topiary a modern twist: waxed pink apples, gilded cones, *Viburnum tinus* berries, and sprigs of red skimmia and pink heads of hellebores top a heavy gilded iron urn.

FAR RIGHT Ornamental kales, camellia leaves, and skimmia form the base of this conical topiary, with pale pink 'Sweet Avalanche+' and 'Aqua!' roses and wired miniature aubergines forming the color accents. Wands of pussy willow add shape and structure.

**GLASS** Simple clear glass is so versatile and I always think it is lovely to be able to appreciate the full value of the flower by seeing the whole stem. It is also fun to personalize clear glass vases by creating your own design with accessories. I collect many useful colored glass pieces, and I particularly love this handbag style by the huge German glass manufacturer Leonardis. I also have many individual handmade pieces, such as this handkerchief vase by Aline Johnson—who, being Dutch, was inspired to make the perfect vase for flower arranging! For me, Aline's use of color is mesmerizing. She takes her inspirations from nature, and particularly the Jurassic coastline of southern England, and so her vases are very empathetic with nature. It is only in recent years that containers have been led by the floral designers and the flower trends, rather than led by a pottery or glass designer designing a vase with scant concern for what the owner would do with it.

ABOVE  A tall tumbler vase contains a single pink lotus flower. I love the fact that you can enjoy the whole flower, stem included, although these rare beauties are sadly short-lived when cut.

RIGHT  A manufactured glass bag vase from the German company Leonardis, filled with dainty pink *Vaccaria hispanica*. This shade of pink combines brilliantly with lime green for a really fresh look.

THIS PAGE A striped Aline Johnson handkerchief vase is filled with pink waterlilies. As well as being a beautiful object in its own right, its shape is perfect for displaying flowers.

pink events

# weddings

Pink is definitely my preferred color for wedding celebrations—I designed my own wedding around the color of the strong mid pink 'Bridal Rose.' Silk-screen printed invitations depicted the chosen flowers: roses, lily of the valley, and a touch of wheat. Wheat was included because my wedding was during harvest time and wheat is such a focus of the landscape where I married in Suffolk, in England's arable agricultural heartland.

OPPOSITE This generous hand-tied bridal bouquet is composed of pink veronica, *Alchemilla mollis*, echinops, 'Sarah Bernhardt' peonies, white scabious, 'Cool Water!' roses, and gray amaranthus. The roses are a perfect match for the fabric of the gown and the gray spiky foliage of the amaranthus and round echinops work well with bluey pinks.

**PERSONAL PREFERENCES** I never force my own taste and likes on customers or clients, and over the years we have decorated weddings in many color schemes. For the first ten years of my professional floristry career I actually designed very few pink weddings. In fact, it was not until the beginning of the 21st century that pink became the pre-eminent color for weddings, and to date it is still the most popular. Of course, after fashion and current trends, two of the most important factors determining wedding colors and, in turn, the flowers, is the season and quite simply personal preference. Despite that, I often find that the least girly of clients can turn to pink for her wedding day, because it is the ultimate celebration of frivolity and femininity. Ultimately it is that "princess" day some people have dreamed of for years and years, and pink is the perfect color.

One thing that is a conundrum to me is that despite the fact all brides think they are being very original and individual, often they end up with exactly the same color palette as other brides getting married in the same season. No one in the wedding industry is prescribing a limited color choice, but over 75 percent of brides seem to plump for very similar colors in the same period. Of course, they all have individual twists, and personality, location, and budget all play a part in making each event personal and unique.

THIS PAGE What could be more appropriate? A heart-shaped wedding posy of 'Sweet Akito' roses. The delicate shading of these roses, which are a relatively recent introduction, gives a great sense of depth.

**BRIDAL BOUQUETS** In recent years the overwhelming flower of choice for the bride's bouquet has been roses, and in the main the preferred option has been for a neat, round, lightweight tied bunch in one color, often in white or ivory to match the bridal gown. Personally I prefer a color against most bridal fabrics, especially white or ivory, as it makes a better statement and I feel color makes the overall effect warmer and prettier; pink is perfect for this. If you do not feel that you can go for a strong color then there are all kinds of ways of introducing a hint of color without going the full way. For silvery or gray dress fabric an accent of silver foliage, which is slightly reflective, is a great way of enhancing the compatibility of the flowers with the gown.

THIS PAGE The muted dusty rose
pink shades of *Zantedeschia*
'Aurora', cream 'Talea+' roses,
and pink *Astilbe* 'Erica' are great
for lifting the bouquet from
the wedding gown and creating
a subtle yet warm rosy glow.

THIS PAGE Country weddings suit a little color and I love to do two or three color bouquets for spring and summer casual weddings. Muscari is a very beautiful wedding flower as its shape is so delicate. The mid-blue color combines well with pink, and is as soothing as the color of a perfect blue sky! In this bouquet it is combined with 'Blushing Akito' roses and blue nigella.

**BRIDESMAIDS' POSIES**  You can have a little fun with the bridesmaids' flowers by making them a slightly more unusual shape or by adding accessories. I love to use little bags or colored baskets, which are easy to carry, or an interesting trim, such as a pretty satin ribbon binding or marabou feather trim for a real touch of glamour. Pomanders are lovely, too, for bridesmaids in the 7 to 12 age range. If the maids are younger than that the pomanders can be rather too heavy and get picked up and put down too often, which damages the flower heads. Roses are the easiest to use in small round spherical balls of foam. With mixed flowers it is more difficult to achieve a perfect ball shape, so I recommend picking one type of flower with uniform-sized heads. Soft stems such as spring flowers are more difficult to use and really require wiring, which is not an amateur sport! I think you cannot beat simple hand-tied posies of one type of flower, and my favorites would be pink ranunculus, peonies, sweet peas, or roses.

THIS PAGE  A floral foam ring around a glass pink candelabra is edged with *Alchemilla mollis* and ivy berries and topped with pink and burgundy dahlias with bright pink 'Karl Rosenfield' peonies, 'Milano' roses, and gloriosa lilies. The cube vase seen on the table beyond is filled with a hand-tied posy of the same combination. The Arne Jacobsen chairs have very sexy tight cerise chair covers made by a fashion designer friend, John Crummay.

**WEDDING TABLES** Whatever the occasion or location I think round wedding tables look best-dressed when they are decorated with arrangements which are at different heights, so that the eye is drawn around the room. In grand ballrooms or marquees this is often achieved by using candelabras or tall fluted vases. For long tables, low arrangements can work well, but if the tables are a decent width you can also get some height by using candlesticks or taller containers. Long tables are mostly used to fit a large number of people into a room, and so are often narrow, and fill up quickly when you have added plates and two or three glasses to each place setting. One thing to bear in mind with low arrangements is that you do not want them to be too low or they will be hidden by the glasses, so vases at least 7 inches tall are best. This is why footed glass bowls or urns are hard to beat as containers for events.

RIGHT Cerise wire-edged ribbon around each napkin and an individual bud vase with a cut to hold a name card; this is a pretty detail and a lovely keepsake or favor idea.

THIS PAGE AND OPPOSITE  A bright pink glass cube vase is filled with a hand-tied bouquet of 'Milano' roses, *Alchemilla mollis*, echinops, gloriosa, *Brachyglottis* 'Sunshine,' pink 'Karma Prospero' and 'Karma Choc' dahlias (a detail is shown left), and peonies.

ABOVE  A 'Milano' rose edged with *Brachyglottis* 'Sunshine,' pink hydrangea, and eucalyptus flowers is secured with vibrant pink ribbon.

LEFT  I find the delicacy of this 'Lyvera!' rose simply breathtaking. The pale tones of the ribbon and the napkin perfectly complement its ethereal beauty.

OPPOSITE  Frosted pink ceramic vases are filled with pale pink 'Sarah Bernhardt' peonies, dahlias, and sweet peas, mixed with *Alchemilla mollis* and hydrangea. Stems of pale pink *Clematis montana* var. *rubens* trail over the top for added movement.

A three-tier hexagonal pink wedding cake has been placed on two blocks of floral foam, separated from the icing on the cake by clear cellophane to keep the cake clean and avoid any contamination of the food. Often we would do this at the last minute and use dry green floral foam. The flowers will last at least five hours, maybe eight, depending on the temperature on the day. If you have to do this earlier and you want to use damp floral foam then remove it from the soaking bucket and let it dry out a little before using. When cutting the foam it is vital to make sure it is level to maintain stability, so a small builder's spirit level can be handy.

OPPOSITE The standard roses 'Blushing Akito,' 'Belle Rose,' 'Heaven!,' 'Aqua!,' and 'Lyveria!' have been mixed with the deep pink spray rose 'Magic Pepita.'

*"The combination of pink icing and rosebuds in every shade of pink is just divine—every girl's dream of a fairytale wedding cake!"*

# christenings

The church is booked, the godparents or supporters have been chosen, and now it is time to decide on the decorations for your celebration. Finding a pink christening gown for your baby girl might be a challenging task, but theming the event pink and serving some pink food and drink will not be a problem!

**FAMILY TEA PARTIES** Mostly christening parties are small informal family affairs and so are ideally suited to afternoon tea. Even though from the perception of the world the English are the originators of a "proper afternoon tea," this lovely tradition now has a rather nostalgic feel to it, as it does not seem to fit easily into our modern lifestyle. The celebration of a birth, the naming of a child, or a christening ceremony are a great excuse to get baking and serve up a pretty pink tea. Sweet treats including pink fondant cakes, iced biscuits, ice cream, and jello all make for a pretty pink tabletop. Toast the celebration with a flute of pink Champagne and, of course, a slice of pink christening cake.

For such an occasion I think the flowers should be delicate and small, and so this is a perfect time to use the huge range of commercially cut spray roses. Developed principally for the wedding business and adored by many because they most resemble garden roses, there are now lots of new varieties and colors. 'Gracia,' 'Pepita,' and 'Lydia' all come in many different pale and mid-pink shades, with the strongest colors in 'Magic Pepita' and 'Romantic Pepita.' The fat headed 'Mimi Eden' shown here in the pink gingham basket is in great supply and available all year round. The surprising thing about some of these spray roses is that you can actually get them about 2–3 feet long, and so they make great fillers even in pedestals, and they last really well.

TOP LEFT  Delicate skeletonized pink dyed leaves were tied around a small glass votive filled with *Brachyglottis* 'Sunshine,' *Alchemilla mollis*, and 'Mimi Eden' roses.

LEFT  Pink-striped candy canes tucked into the fabric napkin rings add a jaunty touch to the gingham napkins and are a lovely party favor to take away.

THIS PAGE The gingham theme continues with the basket filled with cream 'Gracia' and pink 'Mimi Eden' spray roses, *Alchemilla mollis*, *Brachyglottis* 'Sunshine' and feverfew flowers. A traditional tiered cake stand holds a tempting array of raspberry cream buns.

*"A baby girl—
the perfect excuse
for a pink party."*

OPPOSITE  Pale pink tulips, white sweet peas, honeysuckle, and dill in a glass vase filled with alphabet candies create a gorgeous scented spring offering. The palest pink mixes well with other pastel colors and this is one of the rare occasions when you find me mixing pale yellow with pink. I adore fuchsia pink with sunflower yellow, and I can work with pale pink and yellow, but somewhere in the mid color range it can all go terribly wrong. So be wary of mixing pink with yellow unless it is in a vibrant multi-colored assortment. Pink and yellow on their own do not always get on!

ABOVE  Felted gray verbascum leaves are wrapped around glass votives tied with ribbon and topped with 'Anna' roses.

RIGHT  These delicious hand-crafted rose petal bundt cakes come from the Ottolenghi food emporium in London.

**ELABORATE DESIGNS** A patterned tablecloth can be fun to use and here we also used patterned plates. This required a decorative bunch of flowers that was also rich in color and texture, so that it could make an impact when placed on such a busy pattern. Large-headed flowers such as the peonies, gerberas, and celosia help this design hold its own with the fabric pattern.

My good friend Gerhard Jenne, the proprietor of Konditor and Cook in London, made these gorgeous multicolored "Magic" cakes. He is a talented bespoke baker and was the originator of this idea, which now has been "borrowed" by many. He also made the rather gorgeous raspberry cream sponge, which when cut creates a checkerboard effect of pink and white sponge cake assembled with raspberry jam and cream. Shut your eyes when you eat it and you could be at the Mad Hatter's Tea Party from the children's classic *Alice in Wonderland*: very appropriate for a christening.

OPPOSITE The napkin detail, which echoes the decoration on the large cake, is constructed from raspberry colored *Dianthus* 'Farida' and pink variegated dracaena leaves.

THIS PAGE The vase is filled with 'Leila' gerberas, 'Aqua!' and 'Vampire' roses, dill, peonies, *Cotinus coggygria* 'Royal Purple', celosia, red amaranthus, and sprigs of *Origanum vulgare*.

# children's parties

Children's parties, particularly for the under sevens, are currently going through a big revival. They are usually themed and an industry has grown out of the need to decorate the event. However, if all that manufactured plastic and paper gets you down you can find some simple and inexpensive ways to make your party look original, fresh, and pretty.

**DECORATING THE TABLE** After you have chosen your theme then I would pick out your basics before selecting your flowers. There are great disposable napkins, cups, and tablecloths available so you can easily find colors to complement your theme. I found these pink bugs on a flower wholesale internet site and my sundries wholesaler sells the pretty butterflies. Instead of covering the tops of the pink glass plant pot with moss I used some shredded pink paper, but you could also use highly colored sisal, which is widely available from wholesale markets or even good stationers. I chose bubble-gum pink pelargoniums as they were the perfect color, and also inexpensive, and they could be recycled after the event. The butterflies and bugs I reuse as present trim when I am wrapping gifts. Perfect for today's eco-conscious parents!

OPPOSITE A pink table with iced cakes, cookies, and pink milkshakes—sustenance for a group of apprentice fairies. The plastic chairs I bought in a yard sale; they were a municipal brown color and so I spray-painted them pink. The paint ended up costing more than the chairs, but we had fun doing it and they look great!

BELOW Scrumptious homemade strawberry ice cream and berries with pink sugar crystals. I have been known to wander through Fortnum and Mason, the grand food store in London, wondering who needs sugar crystals in such a range of colors, but now I understand why.

ABOVE These bugs came on bamboo canes and the butterflies were also wired, but you could easily wire them yourself so they can be arranged around a plant.

ABOVE A pale pink iced cupcake with a silver foil-wrapped heart-shaped chocolate. What little girl could resist these treats?

RIGHT Pink glass flowerpots are filled with hand-tied posies of high summer garden blooms, including sweet peas, 'Dorothy Perkins' roses, and lavender. Old glass jelly jars edged with string are lined with translucent flower petals.

*"Scented garden flowers and cupcakes are essential party pieces."*

**OUTDOOR EXTRAVAGANZA** Children love eating outdoors, and it saves on the clearing up and mopping of the floors as you can leave all the crumbs for the birds! These little sand-filled glasses are a fun activity to do with little ones as it is easy and makes for a very attractive colorful container. It is best to invest in some plastic funnels so that the children will find it easier to place the sand between the glass and an inner plastic or paper cup. Colorful sand like this is easy to obtain as most pet shops have a wide variety in their aquatic departments. If you then fill the inner container with floral foam you could also get your little ones to fill them with flowers. Using foam is easier and more fun for children than attempting hand tying, and you may be surprised how successful their early attempts at floristry may be.

LEFT  Gold confetti stars have been placed on the blue paper tablecloth to give the party a little more sparkle.

BELOW  A small arrangement to top the cake has been created using the bottom of a disposable plastic cup inset with a tiny block of foam, and then a few matching flower heads have been added.

THIS PAGE For a children's summer outdoor birthday party, mixed posies of *Alchemilla mollis*, deep pink 'Beauty by Oger' roses, yellow achillea, and bright pink 'Amalia' and 'Yellow Dot' spray roses have been placed in two glass tumblers. The smaller one inside holds the bouquet and the water, while swirls of brightly colored aquatic grit to match the flowers have been carefully poured into the outer cavity.

# parties for grown-ups

Roses are the floral equivalent of the little black dress:
they can be dressed up or down, and are the perfect
choice for a grown-up party, whether it be an intimate
get-together at home or a larger, catered event.

**THE VERSATILITY OF PINK ROSES** Throughout the pages of
this book you will see at least 50 different shades of pink roses that
we use. The small selection shown here is in the pale to dusty pink
range, and then there are the more vivid and vibrant pinks such as
'Amalia,' 'Tenga Venga,' 'Poison,' and 'Milano.' I love deep pink
roses that are close to red and remind me of lipstick, such as 'Cherry
Lady' and 'King Arthur.' I adore one or two bicolors en masse:
'Carousel' has a pale pink edge; 'N-joy' is darker and more vibrant.
'Blushing Akito' is the slightly deeper mid-pink sister of 'Sweet
Akito' and as they are from the same family as the white 'Akito' they
work well altogether in a pink and white theme. If you are using
flowers in topiary then it is a good idea to use the same size flower
head. At the smaller end of the scale you have 'Ballet,' 'Heaven!,' and
'Barbie', and at the largest end the aptly named 'Titanic.'

**COCKTAIL HOUR** There are so many great pink cocktails, with or without alcohol, that it is a great theme for a get-together to celebrate a birthday. Professionally, I am often asked to decorate cocktail parties and generally we do some large arrangements for the bar area and small arrangements for the occasional tables. At large cocktail parties the guests usually stand for the three hours they are sipping cocktails, and so it is better to have tall flowers on tables, pedestals or the bar where they can be admired. The flowers need to be above eye level to have impact. Simple but dramatic arrangements work best, and we very often work with lighting companies who give the odd wall or column a pink glow. Pink is a flattering, warming color and works well in many different environments, from the modern to the classic.

RIGHT A flared pink glass table vase makes an elegant shape topped with a large ball of floral foam filled with a tightly massed mushroom shape of 'Sarah Bernhardt' and 'Karl Rosenfield' peonies and 'Milano,' 'Belle Rose,' 'Two Faces+,' and 'Vendelle' roses.

OPPOSITE, LEFT 'Christian' spray roses are laid in a bright pink gift box lined with rosebud-sprigged fabric.

OPPOSITE, INSET Pomegranate Cosmopolitans and Strawberry Daiquiris are served on a pink tray, topped with kitsch but cool cocktail umbrellas, to get the party started.

ABOVE A small votive glass with galax leaf trim and tied with pale pink aluminum wire is topped with a 'Bridal Kimsey' mini gerbera.

OPPOSITE AND LEFT These "birthday cake" arrangements trimmed with candles are very popular for adult birthday parties. Pale pink 'Gerrie Hoek' dahlias and 'Bridal Kimsey' mini gerberas (detail shown left), along with 'Luxuria!' roses, are massed on a base of floral foam in a plastic tray. The container is edged with double-sided tape on which galax leaves are pressed, and secured with aluminum wire. Raised up on a footed pink cake stand and filled with small taper candles, it is just waiting for the birthday girl to make a wish.

# afternoon tea

Stopping for afternoon tea on a regular working day is not something we tend to indulge in these days. But if you have something to celebrate, or want a focus when meeting up with a group of old friends, what could be nicer? It should be a civilized affair, with chintz, pretty china, lace tablecloths, meringues, strawberries, clotted cream, and pretty cupcakes.

THIS PAGE A basket filled with carpet moss and topped with some old garden favorites, such as *Dianthus* 'Monica Wyatt,' border spray carnations, chrysanthemums, and some single pink aster daisies, with feverfew, *Alchemillia mollis* and a touch of double pink eustoma.

OPPOSITE These delicately speckled miniature strawberry and rose petal meringues are a perfect bite-sized treat at teatime, and they look so pretty on a plate.

*"Daisies, dianthus, strawberries and meringues—ingredients for the perfect summer tea."*

**EDIBLE TREATS** The traditional value of afternoon tea mixes well with classical flowers or arrangements with a slightly retro feel. The comfort of a home-cooked iced cake needs to be matched with a simple arrangement of classic flowers. Basket arrangements, simple old-fashioned roses, and arrangements with a light-hearted whimsical feel are just perfect for the revival of this enjoyable tradition. With or without tea, in the last five years there has been a huge resurgence of interest in the cupcake. They used to be decidedly an afternoon treat, but since cupcakes were immortalized in the TV drama *Sex and the City* where the girls enjoyed them at the now famous Magnolia Bakery in New York City, cupcake emporia have sprung up everywhere and eating them is no longer confined to afternoons. I think the attraction is in part the power of color. Who can resist a pretty iced cake? It is decadence and fantasy in an individual paper wrapper. Visually pleasing, nostalgically reminiscent of more secure times, cupcakes are a kind of therapy on a plate, an instant pick-me-up from the trials of everyday life.

OPPOSITE 'Princess Alexandra' garden roses are massed together in a matching rubber vase. I really enjoy mixing the old with the new by taking an old-fashioned rose and putting it into a vase made from a vibrant new material.

RIGHT Frivolity and femininity are the hallmarks of this table setting. Delicate rose pink icing forms a design on these miniature handbag cookies, while heart-shaped sugar sprinkles in deeper shades echo the flamboyance of the roses.

LEFT  When I spotted these ceramic pink waffle cone vases in a shop I thought they would be perfect for a floral take on the quintessentially English ice cream known as a "99," which consists of a chocolate flake placed into an ice cream cone. Here the appropriately named pink 'Barbie' and green 'Peppermint' roses have been arranged in foam to look like dollops of ice cream on a cone.

**TEA BENEATH THE TREES** For this buffet table set out for a celebratory tea I chose a bright pink cloth to add a splash of color to this green spot. Fruit trees, and in particular apple trees, are perfect for hanging votives as they generally have lots of low horizontal branches. We often use the orchard part of the garden for a feature because these trees look so stunning when they are twinkling in the late afternoon shadows. Bright pink votives add to the pink theme and look very pretty as the light falls and all the candles are lit. I particularly like to use scented flowers in my own home and an outdoor party is the perfect time to use flowers that might be quite overpowering in a confined space. Certain fragrances evoke memories and I adore the scent of large oriental lilies that remind me of my own wedding day.

ABOVE LEFT Cakes can be easily dressed up by adding a small floral arrangement to the top. Usually I place a small piece of floral foam in the bottom of a plastic cup. Here I have added weigela, ranunculus, astrantia, and pale pink rose buds.

ABOVE RIGHT The strong colors of these deep pink lilies and chrysanthemums stands up well in bright sunlight, so they are perfect for outdoor arrangements.

LEFT  A blown 'Kansas' peony looks stunning in a matching pink tea glass.

BELOW  Gold and pink is an unusual combination and gives a lovely light to any event. I am always on the lookout for small containers and shot glasses to make interesting votives.

OPPOSITE  A floral ring around a glass bowl of floating candles is made up of grouped gloriosia, bright pink 'Milano' roses, 'Kansas' peonies, orange 'Colandro' roses, orange 'Tango' leucospermums, 'Lill Orange' zinnias, and yellow *Achillea* 'Moonshine' with *Viburnum opulus* berries and *Corylus maxima* 'Red Filbert.'

# dinner parties

Hot pinks are a great color for dinner parties as they can be themed with the food and look good in candle or artificial light. Here, pink and gold Moroccan tea lights set the theme for a North African feast.

**EXOTIC ELEGANCE**  Hot pink can look very sophisticated and I return often to this color because it gives a cheerful and rosy glow to evening light. When it is used with other bold colors it can also be very masculine and so I think it suits lots of different occasions. Hot pink with purple and lime green has long been one of my favorite color combinations, and it is always a safe option, evoking memories of country gardens. Using pink with orange and yellow requires rather more skill, and one tip is to use groups of colors as I have here, with berried foliages such as the *Viburnum opulus* and also some dark burgundy or brown foliages. Here the brown *Corylus maxima* 'Red Filbert' helps to make the bright combinations get along well together.

OPPOSITE *Achillea* 'Moonshine', orange zinnias, and 'Colandro' roses with pink 'Milano' roses, gloriosa, and celosia. The fluffy patches are the tops of *Cotinus*, or the smoke bush, which enhance the texture of this arrangement. This hand-tied posy is arranged in a moisture-containing pink gel that looks like ice, which is produced especially for the flower trade. I am not a huge fan of it, but I like the ice effect of the clear gel and the pink is smart for dinner parties. Be very careful when you dispose of this gel because it is very absorbant and can block sinks and drains.

THIS PAGE One of my all-time favorite flowers is this *Gloriosa superba* 'Rothschildiana'—it is a fantastic color and shape, and often acts as a muse for my flower arrangement.

THIS PAGE A pale pink leather hatbox was filled with 'Milano,' 'Two Faces+,' 'Beauty by Oger,' and 'Pink Avalanche+' roses, augmented with green hydrangea, *Viburnum opulus* 'Roseum,' and ivy.

**ROMANTIC DINNERS** For Valentine's day we have often used hat boxes as containers, which I think is a very smart way to receive a gift of flowers. Here the hat box is filled with an arrangement of hydrangea, roses, and *Viburnum opulus* 'Roseum' to create a perfect pink centerpiece for a dinner party. Stemmed glass bowls and cake stands provide the perfect height for a dining arrangement as they elevate the flowers so that the glasses do not hide them, and still enable the guests to see across the table over the top of the flowers. It is important when planning an intimate dinner that the design does not create a hedge across the middle of the table and that arrangements are not intrusive. They should contribute to the romantic atmosphere, rather than hindering it!

THIS PAGE A glass cake stand has been filled with champagne pink glass beads to hide the floral foam. *Viburnum opulus* 'Roseum' flower heads have been laid on the napkins and a dusting of pink petals strewn across the table. Stemmed bowls and cake stands also allow lots of space for votives, which adds to their suitability as containers for intimate dinners.

*"Candlelit tables on a balmy evening set the scene for a magical dining experience."*

OPPOSITE Black wrought-iron candelabra are the perfect height for a low centerpiece as they are footed and just tall enough to be seen above the wine and water glasses. Grapes have been wired into the bottom of these arrangements with 'Con Amore' roses, 'Cool Water!,' 'Blue Pacific,' and 'Christian' spray roses, along with *Heuchera* 'Plum Pudding' and *Cotinus coggygria* 'Royal Purple.'

THIS PAGE Napkins are trimmed with a 'Blue Pacific' rose and striped voile ribbon and laid on lilac glass serving plates.

techniques

# hand-tied bouquets

THIS PAGE When the stems are cleaned take one central flower between your thumb and your first finger so that it is resting on the palm of your hand. As I am right handed I arrange into my left hand so that my right is available for twisting the bunch and using the scissors for cutting the stems and tie. The second stem will be placed left of the first stem towards a 45-degree angle. After five flowers, use your right hand to twist the bunch and then add another five towards the left at the same angle. What starts off as a fan of flowers will become a spiraled bunch. Continue the same method, twisting as you go, until you have used all your flowers and you will have a lovely dome-shaped bunch. These 'Amalia' roses have then been tied where they were held, which is known as the 'binding point.'

THE PRINCIPLE OF hand tying material started with early farming when sheaves of wheat and barley were spiraled into bunches, which when tied would stand on their own stems and could be left in the field to dry in the sun after the summer harvest. Hand tying flowers began in continental Europe in the later part of the 20th century and was slowly introduced to the UK around 20 years ago; it has since become a familiar floral technique worldwide. It is worth spending a little time learning this skill, even if you do not plan to work commercially with flowers, because you can achieve a very sophisticated look with the minimum of effort. It may take you around three or so goes at spiraling the stems before you get the knack. The best way to begin is with a collection of straight-sided woody stems such as a dozen commercially grown roses. The trade secret to making a great spiraled bunch is all in the preparation. The stems must be cleaned thoroughly so that there is no foliage on the lower stems, and you can use a sharp vegetable knife to prize away any thorns from the stems.

ABOVE LEFT The average hand-tied bouquet consists of around 20 to 30 stems of flowers and foliages with around one third being foliage. Here a summer collection of garden roses, sweet peas, and nigella shows the beginning of a foliage edging or collar. Pinkish dracaena leaves have been folded around the bouquet. You can see how the angle of the flowers gets greater – at the end the bouquet's flowers are nearer a 90-degree angle than the inner circle of 45 degrees.

BELOW LEFT This pastel hand-tied bouquet of gerberas, bergamot, celosia, and roses has been edged with hosta leaves. You can also create a bubble by tying a square of strong cellophane around the straight cut stems and then filling it with water to create an aqua pack. This is the perfect wrapping for a hostess bouquet so that she does not have to search round for a vase just when her guests are arriving!

AN EMPLOYEE OF the Firestone tire factory in the United States accidentally discovered floral foam. The widespread production of the green foam that holds water has now been taken over by the company called Smithers Oasis, and now the green foam has become synonymous with the name "Oasis." Its invention has radically changed the way flowers can be arranged. Usually it is sold in blocks about the size of a house brick, but you can get jumbo blocks for larger arrangements and a huge range of spheres, cones, rings, and other more specific shapes. It is principally dark green, which is generally thought to be the best color as it can be easily hidden by foliage. Do not use the brown foam, which is intended for dried flowers and is not so absorbent. Remember when using foam to soak it for about ten minutes, letting it naturally fall to the bottom of deep water in a bucket or sink. Wait to use the foam until you see that the air bubbles have ceased to rise. Never force it into the water as "drowning" causes air locks to form in the middle. Use flower food as it will improve longevity of the flowers and top up the water mixed with flower food daily. Never let the foam dry out, as it will start to draw the moisture from the flowers and literally suck the life out of your arrangement!

ABOVE LEFT  Balls of foam are useful for formal structures, especially for weddings. When massing lots of flowers it is a good idea to cover the foam with one-inch chicken wire. You can see that this floral foam ball has a plastic mesh around it to prevent it from breaking up when all the flower stems are added. When creating an arrangement like this, cut the flower stems quite short, approximately 2 inches, to avoid them crossing in the center of the foam ball. This vase has been filled with petals and cellophane and topped with 'Revival' roses.

BELOW LEFT  Lime green floral foam has been used here to create a candle arrangement. Make sure you use a lot of floral foam for a candle arrangement and that it rises at least an inch, preferably 2 inches, from the top of the vase so that you can add the flowers and foliage at right angles, as shown here. The candle has been anchored in with bamboo canes, sold in garden centers, or you can use kebab sticks. Floral foam tape secures the canes.

# fixing with floral foam

THIS PAGE One of my favorite floral foam items are rings commonly sold as wreath frames for the sympathy flower trade. These plastic or Styrofoam backed pieces are fantastic for table centers as they come in a huge array of sizes and can be used around vases, storm lanterns, and also candelabras. Here I have backed a 14-inch ring with galax leaves and used cotinus, ornamental kales, hydrangea, and gerberas for decoration. The glass doughnuts seen in the bowl filled with gerbera heads are also useful for floating flowers and protecting them from the heat and flame of lit floating candles.

ALTHOUGH FLORAL FOAM is a great invention, there are times when you need to use other methods. Arranging flowers in water with flower food will give better longevity than foam and so for contract flowers, arrangements for the summer, or when we want to get the absolute maximum life from our flowers we may use methods other than foam. This can also be dictated by the flowers themselves—some varieties do not last well in foam. This especially applies to weak stems such as sweet peas or cosmos, and succulent ones such as tulips, hyacinths, and other spring-flowering bulbs. Hollow stems such as amaryllis and hydrangea will also benefit from being arranged in water, as will thirsty drinkers such as anemones or sunflowers.

ABOVE RIGHT For larger vases, baskets, and also large pedestals I use 2-inch chicken wire to arrange flowers. I scrunch this up so that it fits the container so tightly you can pick up the vase by the wire.

BELOW I am not a great fan of floral gel, but as they make it in great colors, including pink, I thought it would be good to use it here. The gel is made by adding some crystals to water until it expands. As it contains water it allows the flowers to drink, and because of its glutinous quality it keeps stems in place. The clear version is useful for creating an ice effect and gel is really a decorative accessory rather than a simple flower-arranging aid. These crystals last for ages, but are relatively expensive to purchase and have to be disposed of very carefully, as they can seriously block drains and sinks.

# aids to arranging flowers

THIS PAGE  If I am using a delicate shallow container I often use a grid of Sellotape or floral foam. Thin Sellotape works well for glass vases as it is see-through. I usually place all the horizontal pieces first and then add the vertical lines. For this arrangement I balanced bunches of delicate flowers such as the gypsophila with large flower heads of peonies and hydrangea.

# decoration outside a container

THIS PAGE Double-sided tape has been placed around a straight-sided bowl and then sprigs of freshly cut 'Hidcote' lavender has been delicately placed around with the flower heads all at the same height. You can see that we have tied some string around it to assist us. Often we use a large rubber band on large bowls so that we can pull the band out to place each sprig in place behind it, stuck to the double-sided tape.

**IF YOU DECORATE** your container so that it is in sympathy with the flower arrangement you get a much more sculptural effect, and this has become very much part of my signature style. In the days before there were so many floral accessories available, when I started my flower business, there were lots of ugly plastic containers on the shelves at the floral sundries stores. These seemed to me to be at complete odds with the beauty of the flowers. With a little double-sided tape and a few strong glossy leaves such as rhododendron, laurel, galax, or even aspidistra you could transform your plastic inexpensively and quickly and make a natural container. Leaves last around five days before they start to get quite brittle, but mostly they dry out and look fine. For special occasions we have started to use herbs, and rosemary is one of the most versatile because it is around all year. Spruce works well for Christmas and, of course, the fall leaves of oak are perfect. For winter we often get out the hot glue gun and stick cinnamon around plastic bowls. The only limit to this is your imagination and over the years we have tried a variety of natural items, from turnips and leeks to sunflower heads.

ABOVE LEFT With small containers such as votives you can often get away without using any tape by just wrapping three leaves around the outside, and using a decorative tie to keep the leaves in place. These skeletonized leaves are available in a number of dyed colors, as well as natural forms.

BELOW LEFT Pink-dyed decorative twigs have been secured onto a glass vase with double-sided tape, trimmed to size and tied with fuchsia raffia.

# decoration inside a container

BELOW  Two straight-sided glass dishes have been placed inside one another to allow a small gap for a row of candies.  It is important that the gap is wide enough for one layer and not too wide as this makes the cost of the candy filling more exorbitant than the flowers! Here I have used three blocks of colored floral foam to fill the container. Notice that the foam rises about 2 inches above the container, which allows room for a generous amount of plant material and will allow flowers and foliages to be added at right angles so they hang over the edge of the container.

RIGHT  The 6-inch cube vase is one of my favorite containers. It is useful to buy a collection from 4 inches up to 8 inches so you use them in lots of different ways. Here decorative aggregate has been used. By using a central glass container you can add water with flower food to the center vessel so that the grit does not get wet. This way it can be stored and reused over and over.

BELOW A cylinder has been placed inside a fishbowl and then into the space swirls of pink dyed aquatic grit and paler pink colored sand have been added in uneven stripes to evoke the waves of the sea. To achieve the best effect, with clearly delineated waves, use a funnel to pour the grit and sand into the narrow gap.

I HAVE ALWAYS LOVED to customize my own containers and over the years this has become quite a trademark. Initially I used plastic containers that were generally covered on the outside with double-sided tape, but as more and more fabulous glass shapes became available I started to use a container within a container to create lots of different effects. Sometimes the accessory can just add a color, and colored sand and aquatic grit—particularly for its garish colors—has been a huge favorite. Natural reeds and bamboos are great for simple table arrangements and fruit looks great for summer weddings, fall events and, of course, Christmas, with cranberries or sliced oranges being my favorite. Spices such as star anise and cinnamon are also great for the festive season and give off a fabulous fragrance. For themed events, such as children's parties and christenings, I often like to use candies, mainly because I am inspired by their colors!

BELOW Mikado sticks are generally natural and are used by florists in lots of different ways. Here pink dyed sticks have been used to line a container that has been filled with white floral foam to take lines of rose heads—a design suitable for a dining or coffee table. The foam and sticks have been cut just above the top of the container.

# pink flower directory

# pastel pinks

There are numerous shades of pastel pink flowers available all the year round, but many of my favorites are seasonal, and these are most prolific between the months of March and July.

**Protea** (left) The giant king protea is one of the largest pink flowers. Although they are quite expensive to purchase they are worth their cost because they last for a very long time and just a single stem in the right sturdy vase can cause quite a stir. We use them in contract vases, particularly in the summer, because they withstand hotter temperatures.

**Valerian** (1) This is actually a rather dominant self-sown plant in my garden, but I have come to adore these delicate flowers as fillers in bouquets and vase arrangements. This makes a better cut flower than you might expect if arranged in water with flower food.

**Dog rose** (2) These wild dog roses are a familiar site in hedgerows around the area where I live and they remind me very much of long hazy summer days in the country. Single roses have been having a little revival recently and apart from their wonderful shape I adore this shade of very pale pink.

**Lupin** (3) These quintessential garden flowers can often be overlooked as a cut flower because they do not travel very well and tend to drop quite easily. However, I find if I cut them from my garden early in the morning and condition them with flower food they can easily last the best part of five days.

**Clematis** (4) Not yet grown in great numbers as a cut flower, the clematis has been sadly overlooked and rather underrated by the commercial flower industry. These flowers are lovely for wedding work and natural arrangements, when they can trail over the edge of vases and baskets. I like the strength of the vine and the leaf shape, too.

**Anthurium** (5) These funny looking waxy flowers usually divide people into the love or hate camp, but while I did not take enormously to the tropical red varieties I find myself increasingly beguiled by the new varieties and sizes, and I love their vase life habit of a minimum of 14 days to a maximum of 50!

**Sweet pea** (6) Fragrant and delicate, these flowers are among my top ten. Commercially grown sweet peas last longer than those cut from your garden because they are treated after they have been harvested. There is a huge variation in colors and also many bicolors. They last better in water than foam.

**Hollyhock** (7) This quintessential cottage garden flower is grown in small quantities for the cut-flower industry and mainly double varieties are available for a limited season. Unfortunately this flower does not survive well as a cut flower and so I only use them for large arrangements for special occasions such as weddings, and I admire them in my garden.

**Cymbidium orchid** (8) These strong, long-lasting flowers are at their best in the winter and come in a huge range of pinks. The noses are most often burgundy and all have a touch of yellow. The large-headed varieties have 20 or so heads on the stem and can be as long as 2½ feet.

**Honeysuckle** (9) No garden would be complete in my opinion without at least one variety of this plant and I have at least five different varieties so that I can enjoy this sweet musky fragrance for longer. Not a great cut flower, it will not survive floral foam, but it is lovely for special occasions.

1

2

3

4

5

6

7

8

9

# bright pinks

My favorites in the pink palette are the showy, loud pinks that make a strong visual statement.

**Celosia** (left) The vivid rich colors of celosia and their lovely texture provide interest in densely packed bouquets and arrangements. In early summer huge heads of celosia on giant stems are gown around San Remo in Italy and these are fantastic for pedestal designs and large-scale arrangements.

**Peony** (1) Peonies are quintessential blowsy showy pink flowers and have the added advantage of being fragrant. 'Karl Rosenfield' and 'Kansas' are two of my favorite bright pink varieties to use as long-lasting cut flowers.

**Rhododendron** (2) For a very short season in spring I love to use the beautiful flowers from these magnificent shrubs. Their close relatives, the azaleas, sport some beautiful blossoms and also some pretty racy pink colors.

**Stock** (3) This has been a cottage garden favorite for centuries, but has now been much improved. Most widely available is the bright pink *Matthiola incana* 'Francesca.' Pictured here is 'Lucinda Rose.' It also smells incredible.

**Gerbera** (4) These are very versatile flowers available in a huge palette of pink. Among the large flower varieties 'Serena' pictured here is the most common, and 'Whisper' and 'Leila' are my favorite mini gerberas.

**Dianthus** (5) The standard carnations come in a huge array of pink colors and I love the ones that are the closest to purple. 'Farida' shown here is almost the color of beetroot. Massed together, standard carnations are very textural and I prefer to use them cut short in domed hand-tied bouquets.

**Phalaenopsis orchid** (6) Beautiful moth-shaped flower heads in a huge spectrum of bright pink color. On long drooping stems they make exotic but simple bridal bouquets or luxurious vase arrangements. Usually quite pricy, they last incredibly well and so are better value than you might think.

**Tulip** (7) There are a huge variety of pink tulips, including the later flowering 'Pink Diamond,' the fringed 'Huis ten Bosch' and the lily-flowering 'China Pink.' Versatile and easy to use, tulips grow around a third more after they have been cut, so allow for a little movement when mixing with other flowers.

**Dahlia** (8) I adore dahlias for their color and their texture. The Karma series has several pinks and are long-lasting cut flowers. *Dahlia* 'Onesta' is another fine showy pink dahlia. I look out for the Cactus varieties, such as 'Pink Jupiter' or 'Pink Symbol.'

**Fuchsia** (9) No discussion on showy pink flowers should leave out fuchsias, which have so aptly left their mark on the color pink by defining one of its best palettes. Not reliable at all as a cut flower, but an essential part of a British summer either in the garden and on the patio or hanging from a basket.

# mixed pinks

Two-tone pinks are lovely for monochromatic and complementary combinations, and can be visually stunning when arranged on their own.

**Nigella** (left) I saw this exciting new variety, 'Power Pink,' for the first time as a cut flower while we were making this book. The blue cultivar is the traditional color and a cottage garden favorite. I love nigella for weddings in the summer.

**Gladioli** (1) Loved or hated, this sturdy flower is great for large pedestals and for massing in vases. The bicolors and the stronger pinks are my favorites and they last extremely well.

**Zantedeschia** (2) Known more commonly as arum or calla lilies, these elegant long-lasting versatile flowers are the supermodels of the flower industry. They are the flower of choice for many floral designers, so they can usually command high rates because they are always in demand.

**Digitalis** (3) From late April to May, foxgloves grow wild in woods and are very precious to me. I grow some cultivars in my garden and make the most of the limited supply of cut foxgloves when they are in season in May.

**Dianthus** (4) These old-fashioned cottage garden "pinks" have a divine scent and have been admired in English gardens since Tudor times. Their more common supermarket sisters always seem to get a bad press nowadays, but they are hard-working and faithful flowers.

**Gloriosa** (5) This is another top ten flower. I just love its shape, its color, and it is definitely a muse for my inspiration. The bicolor often leads me to use pink with yellow or lime green to some stunning, vibrant effects. It is also another great favorite of mine for use in dramatic wedding arrangements.

**Lily** (6) There are so many great pink oriental lilies around and I always like to have a vase on the go at home. They last for up to two weeks and they give off a divine sweet smell that reminds me of my wedding day.

**Mallow** (7) This lowly common pink flower often found on roadsides or wastelands has many famous pink relatives, from the lofty hollyhock to the tropical hibiscus. It has beautiful delicate rose-purple flowers which have been admired since the 8th century, and has been used widely as a medicine and a food as well as a cut flower.

**Astrantia** (8) Some flowers are all about the color, others scent, but this one is all about the texture. The delicate umbrella-shaped heads make great supporting actresses to roses in summer wedding bouquets. They enhance other shapes and last well themselves.

**Rose** (9) There are lots of bicolor roses from the garden as well as commercially grown cultivars. In my garden I grow 'Handel' around an arch and favorites that are commercially grown include the small-headed rose 'N-joy' and the large-headed 'Dolce Vita.'

# index

Figures in italics refer to captions.

# acknowledgments

This book has been an absolute pleasure to work on. It has been a long time in the pipeline, so there has been a huge team that has worked on it or were involved from its conception to its birth. A huge thank you to Jacqui Small, my publisher, for giving me the opportunity to indulge my love of pink! Thanks to her efficient and artistic team, which includes as usual the talented and patient designer Maggie Town, the very capable and knowledgeable skills of my editor Sian Parkhouse, Lesley Felce, and all at Jacqui Small who lent pink props, shared pink insights, and loves and added to the passion for this book as well as to the organization.

A very special thank you to all the photographers who have worked on these pink designs including Sian Irvine and Sarah Cuttle and a very big thank you to Polly Wreford who shot the body of new work for this special and very personal book. Polly and I had worked together once before about 20 years earlier when we were both starting out on our careers and it was an immense privilege and fun to work with her on this project. As usual in publishing these days, she had to achieve a lot in a very short time, which required immense skill, vision, speed, and patience. Heartfelt thanks to Polly and her assistant Sarah.

Over the last 20 years I have had the pleasure to work with lots of lovely talented florists and we have also trained and added to the experiences of many along the way. During the production of this book I have had the pleasure to work with the following talented people:

Wendy Boileau, Heidi Bradshaw, Anne Cadle, Katie Cochrane, Kirsten Dalgleish, Yolanda Davis, Steve Dzingel, Anita Everard, Jason Fielding, Samantha Griffiths, Anna Hudson, Gina Jay, Shontelle Jepson, Anita Kovacevic, Hyunah Lee, Hyun Sook Lee, Su Yeon Lee, Miranda Laraso, Sarah Laugher, Estelle Montlouis, Gillian Munday, Annabel Murray, Tania Newman, Phil O'Neil, Penny Pizey, Ann Pochetty, Hayley Pryke, Joanne Rouse, Chris Sharples, Miki Tanabe, Viktor Tordai, Natasha Tshoukas,   Vilija Vaitilaite, Hisako Watanabe, Karen Weller, Kate Wozniak, and Jisook Yim.

Thank you to our cake bakers Fiona Cairns, Penny Pizey, Gerhard Jenne, and the team at Ottolenghi. Thanks to Anne Cadle for the lovely pink wedding cake on page 86. Thanks to Aline Johnson, Isobel Stanley, and Emma Bridgewater for their creative containers.

My longstanding flower suppliers: in particular in New Covent Garden market and also in the Netherlands. Dennis at John Austin and Co, Marcel from MHG flowers and Kees and Jack from Ros flowers, The team at Bloomfield, everyone at Best, Whittingtons, and Pratleys.

Last but by no means least, a very special thank you to my family who have contributed so much to this project and who are a constant support. Thank you for your love and encouragement.

# picture credits

All photography by Polly Wreford, with the exception of the following pages:

Sarah Cuttle: pages 22, 23, 34, 39, 40, 41, 46, 49, 51, 54, 56, 58-59, 64, 66, 67 (inset), 68 (right), 69, 76, 98–99, 120–21, 139 (top left, center and right), 141 (top left and center)

Sian Irvine: pages 35, 36–37, 38, 42-43, 48, 50, 55 (inset), 65, 67 (right), 84 (inset), 85, 112–13